The Fragrance of Water

Poems by

REUBEN V. GREENE III

Gray Matter Press
Seattle Los Angeles

Copyright © 2025 by Reuben V. Greene III

All rights reserved. No part of this publication may be reproduced, distributed, or transmitted in any form or by any means, including photocopying, recording, or other electronic or mechanical methods, without the prior written permission of the publisher, except in the case of brief quotations embodied in critical reviews and certain other noncommercial uses permitted by copyright law. For permission requests, write to the publisher, addressed "Attention: Permissions," at the website below.

Gray Matter Press
The Brain Initiative, Inc.
www.the-brain-initiative.com

ISBN-13: 979-8-9862415-3-1

The Fragrance of Water
Reuben V. Greene III, 1st ed.

Book design and cover design by Seán Dwyer
Photos courtesy of Jeff Danielson, © 2025

Introduction

Gratitude for all of the manifestations of nature—the flowers, trees, animals, and water, even mountains and clouds that have been ever-present on this life-journey and have spoken their wisdom and given sustenance.

A very special and heartfelt thank you to Seán Dwyer for his guidance and encouragement bringing these pages to print.

Contents

Introduction	v
Not to Die	1
At the End of the Pier	2
Clouds	3
O'Keefe	4
Under the Weather	5
Of the Land	6
The Bird Messenger	7
The Boat	8
The Evening Geese	9
Apex	10
Conversion	11
Sea Song	12
The Great Friend	13
Laughter Not My Own	14
Great Blue Heron	15
October	16
Grace	17
Sacred Sky	18
The Power of Beauty	19
Dragonflies	20
Trust	21
Eyes of Wonder	22

The Fragrance of Water 23
Fellow Traveler 24
The Dance 26
Thirst 27
Sanctus 28
Autumn Pages 29
Nami 30
Shelter 32
Pages Turn 33
Full House 34
Leaning 35
Ether 36
Refuge 37
She Said Call Me Grandma 38
Wings Aflutter 40
Innocence of Babes 41
Pages Turn 42
Tomes 43
Back Then 44
Distillation 45
Jane Kenyon 46
Starling's Song 47
At the Side of the Road 48
Sanctuary 49
The Elders 50

Desert Sanctuary 52
Aunt Cynthia's Sweet Pages 53
New York Deli 54
Temple 56
Benediction 57
Pulse of Early Evening 58
Quiet Desert 60
Stalker 62
The Light 63
Nearly Still 64
Songs Rising 65
Meditation 66
Fort Casey 67
The Squawkers 68
Kinship 69
The Why 70
To the Cormorants, Again 72
Whisper 73
Still 74

The Fragrance of Water

Courtesy Jeff Danielson © 2025

Not to Die

The speaker talked about how crucial,
how painfully necessary it is
not to die with your voice
still deep inside you.
Even when you don't know the combination to the vault;
access to the jewels.

Issues rumbling so far below the surface
you don't know how to reach them.
What do you do?
You persevere! At times, a miracle in itself!

The pain of the search beyond understanding,
Yet, by degree, yielding, bearing fruit.

And you, able to breathe,
really breathe,
perhaps
for the very first time.

At the End of the Pier

The gulls struggle
against the wind
and mussels are now exposed
on rocks and vertical log supports.

Massive planks clunk as I walk,
a giant piano underfoot.

Mountains stretch across the horizon
and they, with water, birds
and shoreline trees
shimmer in the sun.

From the inside wall of the pier café
a picture of steaming coffee on a table
and a spaniel lies on the floor
looking down approvingly.

At the end of a hundred-year-old pier
the past briefly opens on creaking wood
and I travel back in time…
returning to the present…. renewed;
carried by echoes of continuity.

Clouds

They race across
a bracing sky
in groups.

Now three or four together,
now six or eight.
The energy, the colors!

Blue, purple, reds
and some beyond description.
Like families,
holding hands,
dashing together
late for an appointment.

Awed by their mutations,
power and
silent beauty,
I stand quiet
and perfectly still.

O'Keefe

Georgia O'Keefe painted large,
voluptuous, expansive.

The beauty of simplicity,
and the need to pause
to see it.

A rose, a lily, a daisy
shares itself…
form, fragrance
and color…

a healing… to the world.

Offering itself freely,
without condition.

Touching even
beneath the surface
of conscious thought.

Under the Weather

The medication has had a strange effect.
Leaving me somewhere on the edge.
Between wanting to act,
to fill the day, and lethargy.

Open to the suggestion of sleep,
but not entirely.

Frustration raises its hackles
as I feel myself drift,
no momentum to move.

So, I sit in the rocker next to the window
studying the stillness
of the world outside.

Contenting myself
to let what is ….
simply be.

Of the Land

I am of this land
I am its child.
And, when away
am restless
until . . .
in heart and touch
I embrace it once again.

The Bird Messenger

A solitary bird flies onto the branch
of a date palm tree.
Intent and hungry, fluttering about.

Then swooping to the next tree,
he hops from branch to branch...
still nothing to eat.

I watch from an overstuffed chair
in the hotel lounge,
a single soul struggling to survive
in the oppressive desert heat.
Yet, determined and persevering.

A messenger perhaps.
Whispering "Carry on,
Carry on,"
even in the midst
of apparent deprivation.

The Boat

In the distant ocean a lone sailboat
drifts slowly on fall air as wind deliberates.
No motor, no sound,
dependent upon the graces of nature
for movement.

On the pier where I stand
A column of ants parades along
the left border of a flower box
brightened by blue and yellow blossoms.

The flowers… extravagant splash of color,
the boat in gentle drift…
and ants obediently following orders
of an instinctive urge.

All moving rhythmically
with what
God has sent their way.

The Evening Geese

Seven thirty and the geese colony
feeds near the lake.

Just ten feet from my bench,
the young ones peck at grass.
The last feeding before sunset.

They glance at me as I sit in stillness,
at total peace in their world.

Glancing again, on occasion,
they continue feeding.

"Oh, he's the same one who comes here
again and again as if he is one of us," they think.
"Reclaiming at our lake, what his world,
subtly or brutally,
has taken away."

Apex

If one loves the earth,
really
in his bones
loves the earth,
he will have
substantial, soul-searching issues
with the all-consuming
appetites of men.

Conversion

The lone kitten rescued from
the oppressive desert heat
is becoming a cat.
From the withering form I found foraging
alone and motherless, a few months old,
he has grown prodigiously into a regal beauty.

Regular meals, fresh water and a warm bed
have done wonders for an orange and white tabby,
blue eyes and an independent soul.
He won't be dictated to, though time and space
have cultivated affection.

As I put the key into the lock at night,
a lyrical meow rises.
I open the door and there he is
rolling on his back, greeting with play.

There was a time when I thought I couldn't convert;
couldn't accommodate catness.
For a dog-lover, it seemed too alien.

But, there is hope,
even for me.

To learn to love
where I thought
there was no love.

Sea Song

High on a tree branch near the open sea
a russet bird stood alone, but not lonely,
speckling the evening air with song.

So contagious was it that I whistled back.
And with each whistle he trilled multiple notes
as I delighted with this bond.

Eventually walking on I noticed him following.
Not only continuing to sing but facing me all the while.

The uplift of this joy between us
more profound
than any words I could muster
in my entire vocabulary.

The Great Friend

I settle my sack on the sofa
and take the dog out.
Up the hill he pulls and tugs.
He knows where he is going,
smells what I cannot,
hears what is imperceptible to me.

The mysterious and beautiful canine.
Sometimes seeing events before they happen.
Like the dog who, with a nudge, showed a lady
her cancer before it spread.

Teaching without words.
A glance from deep pensive eyes.
A lean into the body… that is a hug.

The heart pounds with gratitude,
as the burdens of the day diminish.
I stop, again, thankful for the gift
of this great friend.

Laughter Not My Own

A huge table of foreign-born ladies
is under the trellis of the café.
Thick wisteria weaves overhead
protecting them from the sun.

Rounds of laughter reverberate as they all join in.
They know one another well and this must be a social club.
Joy rising like helium-filled balloons
or sweet incense.

There is much trouble in the land.
Millions without jobs, homes being lost.
My own situation uncertain.

But for now...for now...
I let the joy next to me lift me above worry
and share the energy of this group that I don't even know.
Yes! I choose to look, see and feel affirmations.
If not my own,
then the joy of others.
Joy is joy, no matter where it comes from.

Great Blue Heron

The days of the month pass much too quickly.
Autumn already and the air whips its chill more and more.
The great blue heron now stands in the stream behind the
    house.
His substantial shoulders in a crouch, immobile.
Long, stilt-like legs anchored in the water's soft bottom.

He must be waiting for something to swim by.
Not even a twitch; eyes frozen, long beak pointed straight
    ahead.
His blue chest and slate wings noble and proud.

I watch him carefully.
A composite of extreme features blend into one handsome
    creature.
I wonder if he will eat tonight, and it is getting late.

Then, like a dance, his expansive wings make a soft but
    powerful whoosh.
and in two or three immense flaps he is in flight.
A beautiful, lyrical sight; is there anything more
    breathtaking!

He heads toward the full moon that will be his evening
    companion.

Goodbye, dear friend.
Though you tried hard,
It seems you will go unfed tonight.

October

Mid-October;
and an invasion
of heat has hung heavy
for the past few days.

But now,
the gift!
Weepy skies,
cool winds
and a stillness
in the heart
despite the challenges
of societal insanity
rising like Mt. McKinley.

Still, I am here,
I have this day,
that in itself, a gift.
So I grasp
whatever it sends my way.

    ....as I did with a fall yellow pear plucked from a wooden crate at the country market.

Grace

The blazing gold
of the heavens
the ultimate life force.

Lifting all it touches,
Speaking in warmth
even to the very depths
of darkness.

A God grace
that saves
those losing hope,
or without even
the slightest trace
of it.

I reach for it.
Feel it flow in and through.
Seeing, feeling
how it saves.

Sacred Sky

A field of clouds
pushed here, then there
by determined winds
telling a story
all their own…
a mystery
with an ending
I will never know.

The Power of Beauty

Silken clouds
hang luminous
in the evening sky.
Shining hope
beyond the limits
of my vision.

Miraculous clouds
taking me with them.
Once more
out of my head
of worries.

Dragonflies

They would usually come in groups
of three or four.
In the scorching desert,
shimmering reds, blues, purples and colors
I couldn't identify.
Angel-like and willowy, hovering on twin sets of silken
wings.

They rested on flowers and watched,
as if in visitation.
At times, among the flowers,
they'd come almost to my face,
turning their heads side to side,
gently observing.

Doubtless feeling my invitation
for them and the peace they brought
on wings of light,
and their essential link
in the great plan
of creation.

Trust

Now there are eight birds sitting on the wall,
an increase of two, at peace in the soft rain.
How does one learn to live by silent guidance
as the animals do?

The birds don't seem to struggle or grimace.
Though only God knows their thoughts.
To my mind they seem content,
not fretful or fearful about tomorrow.

Much of what is true is silent.
Do the birds have implicit trust?
Like my dog, deeply intuitive,
who doesn't know how
I will take care of her.
But, in her trusting heart,
has ultimate faith
that I will.

Eyes of Wonder

When a little boy,
six or seven,
walks up to a café window
in the rain
and peers at you smiling,
huge eyes of innocence,
you know
you must be doing
something right.

Eyes of wonder
don't lie.

The Fragrance of Water

When I am thirsty,
very thirsty,
I can smell it
even from a distance.

Delicate and rich
like melons …or plums.
Exhilarating, lifting the senses.
Life-giving.

I hear its music,
Inhale its cool vapor.
Sense the life it carries within.

The clear, sweet,
soul nourishing
fragrance
of water.

Fellow Traveler

Much of what I see
I do not understand.

I got in the car to drive towards the woods.
The place where silence speaks beyond words.

On the windshield,
a tiny bug,
still and alone.

I accelerate
and expect him to fly off.
He doesn't.

I'll test him.
I go faster;
he clings even more.

The wind against him
so strong
he vibrates.

But, refuses to let go!
How could this be?
Where does this strength come from?

I accelerate to 60 thinking he will fly off!
Still fighting the wind and vibrating,
he does not give up.

When I get to the woods
and park,
he is still there.

I look at this tiny wonder
unable to fathom,
yet, aware enough to know

forces all around me
that I neither see nor understand
hold this blue gem of a world together.

All manner of fellow travelers with me
on what is akin to a grain of sand called Earth
on a beach stretching to infinity and beyond.

Giving me the eyes of a child
as I rise daily from my bed,
whispering, "Thank you."

The Dance

The wind over the open sea
blows inland, ferocious.

Hard to remain upright
as I return to the car.

A colony of gulls soars in the wind,
rising higher, not flapping,
riding invisible waves.

They circle and return.
What simple yet extravagant display
of freedom!

Looking up,
lost among clouds and soaring wings,
my earthly worries dissolve.

Unable to look away,
not wanting to lose them,
I cling to the gift of their dance.

An elixir in these moments.
Soothing all manner
of discontent.

Thirst

One day inevitably gives birth
to the next.

After the meeting
I drive to the beach
then up to the bluff

From here I walk
on gravel, stones and rocks;
crunchy but massaging underfoot.

The aromatic lift of water rising,
quenching in its effect
my thirst for this place.

The interplay of stone and water
gifting a calm.

Even the play of rocks upon rocks,
rolling over one another beneath my feet,
this, too, a part of the music
of this place.

Sanctus

With the change of seasons,
the river has now
a deep crust of ice.

But, cattle must cross
to winter pasture.

Young ones,
never having crossed,
stop at the edge.

If ice is not deep enough
some could fall through.
Yet, there is little choice.

As they are herded forward, they start.
Haltingly at first, then move ahead;
others follow.

A few hooves crack the ice,
but there is now momentum
from the push of the herd.

All, even the young ones,
make it to dry land.

And, to pasture more meagre
yet nourishing enough to see them through.

As if to celebrate,
frost and cold pause their advance…
hesitating
over far distant hills.

Autumn Pages

Red, gold and russet leaves announce its arrival.
Carpeting the ground almost overnight
and winds from the open sea
blow as if appointed for these days.

Winds and bluster
not announcing ill,
but a necessary turning of
seasons' pages.

Just as sinking into sleep
prepares my tired mind
for the coming day,
one I've not yet seen.

Its kernel of hope like a tiny pinecone
and its embedded, unseen life,
grasped tightly
in my protective hand.

Nami

I tried three or four times without success.
Each time talking to her softly,
bringing gifts,
and sitting low.

On the fifth try
she realized she could trust me
in the broken places
of the heart.

And came to the door
of the enclosure,
as I opened it slowly.
First retreating, but this time returning.

Letting me attach the collar.

We spent almost an hour
on the shelter's wooded trails
and running free
in the expansive grassy field.

Running to exhaustion
for the sheer joy of it,
she came up to me,
ready to return to quarters.

It was a long, deliberate effort,
but worth every moment.

Unseen scars and wounds
take time…heal slowly…
for dogs
and humans alike.

Shelter

Tall, willowy grasses shine
luminous in the
evening sun.

Tilting landward as winds
blow with conviction
from the open sea.

I come to this high bluff often;
away from the world,
as it is.

Yet, there is life here.
I hear birdsong on the wind,
rising from the camouflage of thick bushes and trees.

And a colony of whitetail rabbits
watches from a distance
to see if I am trustworthy.

I want to tell them,
to even the wildflowers
that light up the hills,

that I am.
That I, too, have come here
for shelter.

Pages Turn

The air blows crisp and bracing on the skin as I
slowly breathe in…then out…reconnecting.

Here again and when away too long
I begin to feel the empty spaces within.

Spaces that only this place can fill.

I am of this place
and belong to it,
breathing the essence of waters and trees
that tower beside and above me.

Yet, none of this
belongs to me.

With clarity, I know I am here like the pages of a book
blown forward with increasing speed.

Pages I may fill…while the Unseen Power that moves the
 wind turns them…
despite protests or feeble resistance.
A Power infinitely beyond my naïve efforts to reconfigure
 or control.

Full House

Bright yellow wildflowers
smaller than a penny
light the upward path
along the bluff.

Below, the murmur
of cold evening waves.

Yet, enveloped
in the warmth of this silent place, the heart is at home.

There, not far, a lone bird on a top branch
trills as if for an audience.

There is! An audience of one.
He continues and
I respond, copying his song.

No one here but us two
and yet there is a full house.

A house of two;
hearts in song, filled to overflowing.

Leaning

The evening sea is calm,
A soft murmur rolling over
the waves.

The bluff, though,
tells a different story.

Tall evergreens lean away…
away from the sea.

Living history
of fierce ocean storms
that fashion all impediments
to their will.

There is brutal beauty
in the witness of the trees…the unyielding will to
overcome.

I know deeply what it is
to lean away in the storm.

Like these monuments to perseverance,
to bend low, but remain rooted.
To twist beyond endurance,
Yet still upright, still standing.

Here facing the wind,
I know their story.
Their twisted limbs, by grace,
is my story, too.

Ether

I followed the whisper
of branches on wind
into the dense woods
that enveloped me whole.

Then, a world beyond peace,
lifting on dense aroma.
Expansive vault of branches overhead.
Lifted again, with songs,
of hidden wrens in their nests
such that my feet
scarcely brushed the ground.

Refuge

The wind blows cold across
the open sea and over grassy fields.
All the way to the thick wooded forest.

It is a battle to stay upright,
my head into the wind, my six-foot staff for balance.

Rare today, no grazing deer.
It would be a battle on fragile legs.
They are wise to stay in the woods for cover.

I, too, seek refuge!
But, not from the wind,
for it will pass.

Rather, from the world and its dysfunctions.

So, I come here…
Where even winds
that bring tears to the eyes
give respite from
the increasing storms
of decreasingly civilized men.

She Said Call Me Grandma

It is the 1930's
and in the photo
she sits next to
her mom.

Tall and proud,
she says she loved her mother
and all who worked on the farm
during the horrible days of the Depression.

Unlike many, they didn't suffer,
situated on 1,600 acres.
Providing all they needed for themselves
and others.

She got to live
the life she wanted,
not shackled by
economic necessity.

Now 98, her contentment is visible.
Waiting, she says, for the Lord

to open the gates
and let her in.

No doubt
that they, those who
have gone before,
are waiting for her.

Looking at me pensively she says,
"Don't wait for things
to fall into place.
Be fearless now!

As I juggle a confusion of possibilities
her words, weightier than ever,
come back over and again.
"Don't wait…Leap now."

Wings Aflutter

The birds gather at the beach,
but feeding them is "harassment"
the lady officer
tells me.

Deflated, I put the feed back
into the trunk of the car.
Now, I try to figure out
Plan B.

These days I keep an eye out
for her car.
If she's there, I make the rounds innocently
and leave.

If she's not, the trunk comes open,
and it's feasting from the 40-pound sack
of cracked corn,
especially popular now when the weather's cold.

Gulls, crows, ravens and pigeons,
heads up, wings aflutter.
And strangest of all,
not one of them has complained about harassment.

Innocence of Babes

It is 7:40 and the fishermen
at the pier
have left
for the evening.

It is chilly.
And again, four Canadian Geese families
gather the babes and head for the cover
of thick bushes.

It is good.
Good to see so many goslings
have survived. . .
still fuzzy and yet without feathers.

But time is short.
And feathers will come as they must.
These quiet times a gift,
 amidst the calm of innocence.

Innocence, a balm for the spirit . . .
so needed in these days
of tribulation when up is the new down.

Pages Turn

Autumn has arrived.
Its chill preceding it
by a week or more,
giving notice of its coming.

Skies, more often sullen,
now hang heavy,
clouds brooding and low.

The forest though,
and its dense, moist floor
holds the intense aroma
of pine needles underfoot.

Essence rising on moist air,
lifting even unconscious melancholy
beyond where it imagined
it could be.

Tomes

The minister gave a good sermon,
and I took plenty
of notes.

Much to learn
and maybe more
to let go of.

I drive to the shore,
eager for the encompassing sound
of waves.

Cars are tightly parked
on the narrow road.
Refugees seeking open space and quiet. . .
Most here are here for quiet, too.

The subtle whisper
of wind on waves
every preoccupation
rising like mist. . . into the distant ether.

Back Then

The snow has fallen copiously,
 its silent magic
for the second day in a row.

And, back I go…
when mom rushed to the window
calling the three of us kids
to see transformation newly fallen.

All these years
and still engraved,
the return to magic…

Magic…of a newly silent
and unblemished world.

When the complication of these days weighs upon
these less robust shoulders,
I travel back, again.

To a monochromatic and noiseless world of quiet
 simplicity,
seen again through the widening eyes of
a boy of ten.

Distillation

A simple walk
into the woods.

In the deep, heavy silence,
a clarity.

Beyond even the analyses
of Sigmund Freud
or Carl Jung.

Jane Kenyon

She used words like the brush of a painter.
Perhaps as an impressionist
like Monet used nuance to fill a canvas
from bare to stunning.
When she told a story, even a simple one,
I was lost to myself and carried away...
To a world rich with image; palettes of nuance.
Sometimes, even the richness of despair;
tempered by a hint of hope, a whisper.
Or, the pain of devastating loss.
At forty-eight she fought the villain
but cancer's darkness stole her light.
No clue her husband,
survivor of several surgeries,
would remain to battle alone.
Staring at the mammoth hole of a flowering life cut short.
She left like a deep red rose;
petals heavy with the fragrance of life.
Dropping in slow progression.
One…by one…by one….

Starling's Song

The tiny starling
in the cage,
a companion,
sang daily.

Sharing inspiration and form
to some of Mozart's great art.
Notes on air
lifting him from a dead end.

Like notes on wind
rustling through the trees.
Or the cadence of waves whispering
as I walk along the shore.

The music of a heavy downpour
upon my head
and drops on an outstretched tongue,
a christening.

Even families of clouds, silent to some,
they, too, have their music.
Just ask the stars
their glimmer pulling strings of the heart to heights not
      reached before.

At the Side of the Road

Beyond the flowing wheat field
a lone farmhouse at the end
of a narrow dirt road.

I pull over and stop the car;
turn off the motor
and sit.

In the far distance beyond the farm
a thick curtain of trees stretches
across a hill.

Alone and still in the deep calm,
only the near silence
of my breathing. . . in and out….in and out.

A lone red-winged hawk,
immobile atop a tall wooden pole,
observes in perfect silence.

Sanctuary

The long guns in the hillside
of the abandoned World War fort, still and silent.
Hidden among the camouflage of bushes
overlooking the open sea.

Now, the sound of circling wind
buffets my ears.
A strange calm
among silent canons.

Intermittent notes rise
from birds' nests
hidden in thick, tall grasses
willowy in the air.

All this war machinery,
once the avant-garde of military might,
now a sanctuary
of healing.

Birds, white-tail rabbits and grazing deer,
my fellows here.
At their leisure and unafraid, reclaiming the land.
Calling all this, once more, their own.

The Elders

A lone deer stood there.
In the middle of the country road.

As I got closer, he looked at me,
making no effort to move.
As if I were in his domain.
Of course, I was.

His kin here
long before men
arrived on these shores

So, I owe him the courtesy of respect.
For not having plowed the land.
Or paved it and cut its trees
for pencils and toilet paper.

No construction of office buildings,
or condos;
or match boxes
that hurt the eyes.

He and his fellows in their natural state,
letting the land be…undefiled.

I owe him the courtesy of respect
for honoring
and even nurturing
the land.

I waited a good long while
as he considered…
considered what to do
with me.

After a spell…a long one…
and I had given him his time,
he ambled off slowly to the side of the road
and into the woods.

I turned the key
to start the motor.

Remembering what my dear mom said
more than once to adolescent ears,
"Give respect, unhesitatingly,
where respect is due."

Desert Sanctuary

Wherever I go
the world and its noise
often follow.

It cannot believe
I don't want its latest news
and turns the volume even higher.

Now I see...
Why the Desert Fathers
went off into the far and high mountains.

Where they heard the quiet...and its voice.
Among the sand and hills
and echoes
of the lone wolf.

Aunt Cynthia's Sweet Pages

As a young lady you were tall and slender,
moving to Pennsylvania in a government job
you held until retirement.
Coming to visit family several times a year.

Today, my sister tells me in a letter
you are in a home for elders.
Unable to manage your affairs,
your world getting smaller.

My sister sometimes comes to visit.
When she comes you speak of things
she knows nothing of.
Sometimes you don't know who she is.

Your wondrous creativity now faded.
You no longer prepare
warm family meals
in prodigious quantities.

The patterns for making
shirts and dresses and coats
have been put aside, idle.

Your thoughts and your words
take frequent detours
from a life once rich,
like your handmade lace mantle coverings.

My sister squirms at times
when you question her about
who she is,
and if she knows any of your family.

New York Deli

I step inside
a New York Jewish deli restaurant
right in the heart
of Glendale, California.

Behind the counter is Evelyn,
a philosopher,
spitting off wisdom
at the speed of light.

When her husband started to complain,
she relates,
about her 17 cats and two dogs,
she showed him the door.

They're all spayed and neutered, she relates,
but if she had to do it over
she'd become
a forensic scientist.

"What you're doing for the animals
is much more important", I add.

"Yeah, I'm the St. Francis of Assisi here.
Although, I always thought Francis was a woman.

But, you know,
he was a man."

"I've been here 22 years
and my accent
is still as New York
as the day I left."

As I'm leaving,
I hear her tell a customer,
"I'm a boozer honey. It keeps me
from slapping people around."

A rapid and humorous education
in a New York Deli.
Right in the heart
of Glendale, California.

Temple

I return to visit my old friend, ancient oak.
It's been months since I last sat here
under the umbrella
of its branches.

The relief of subtle breathing,
awareness of my smallness
amidst 250 acres next to a giant
like none other.

A million or more leaves,
branches so long
some lightly sweeping the ground,
enveloping me.

This essence in the air
must be the scent of life,
skin tingling,
shelter from even the slightest care.

Benediction

The Amish say their labor is worship.
Not complaining of what must be done,
but throwing themselves into it.
Dedicating the work to God.

A young wife
in starched bonnet and long dress
cans vegetables
in the kitchen.

Her husband, with wide-brim straw-yellow hat
walks sturdily behind a plow,
drawn by the strength of
a huge dappled horse.

This is the way to God, they say.
The prepared vegetables lined up on the porcelain table.
The rows of scrupulously tilled soil,
dark and rich.

And faith extending to the sky
as far as the eye can see, and beyond.
All of this labor
offered up to an infinite and loving Creator.

Pulse of Early Evening

Water still flows
in the wetlands
as ice forms
its lacy crust
around the ragged rim.

Somber logs wallow
in dark waters
resembling animal bodies
submerged,
floating.

Fall's leaves scatter
on intermittent wind;
a final effort
at free will.

I stand beside
the massive wooden rail
and look for life
through the water's bleakness.
Life lurking in willows and rushes
or just beneath the surface... and deeper.

Nothing moves to my eye.
But the heart pounds,
intuiting nature's silent ones
watching from the comfort
of camouflage.
Spectators to an intruder.

And is it not right
that I should walk softly,
uninvited guest
that I am?

Softly,
to their rhythm.
Softly. . .
in their domain.

Quiet Desert

In late evening I open the album.
I look at photos of sand.
Endless waves that repeat
over and again.

I wonder who's living in my house,
22 kilometres outside of town
and nestled against
the huge broken mountains.

Is anyone putting water out
for Miss Kitty and the little ones,
no doubt scampering
behind her?

The big old tomcat
I called Trouble
must be causing as much devilment
as ever.

I look at a photo of my clothes
out back on the line.

and strung from the mammoth
Eucalyptus tree.

I could have hung them in the laundry room.
But there was something allegorical
about the way they twisted and danced in the wind,
sometimes resembling men in jeans and tee shirts.

Or children reveling in the openness of desert
and its peace.

Where wild animals ambled down the mountains
in the evening's cool to drink
from the community bowl of fresh water
I'd set out for them.

Each evening,
water put out for the wild ones
and their young,
before the late sun went down.

Stalker

What once was
is never exactly the same.

Sunken eyes
deep and blank;
body shrunken to skeletal frame
barely moving.

Food left on the plate till dry.
Hiding behind the chair
to not be seen,
not to frighten.

Every effort I muster
met with blankness.
Regal orange tabby now fading;
eyes once pale blue now pleading.

Feline cancer stalking him.
Stalking me.
Even stalking every room in the house.
Stalking every chamber of my heart.

The Light

When the poet Blake lay dying in his bed;
when his body was somewhere
between this world and the next,
he said he heard angels singing.

I've talked with those
who've been to the other side
and come back to tell
what they've seen and heard.

When pilgrims have reached
and seen the Light
and brought back messages for ears unplugged,
I take notice.

I listen.
And take heed.

Nearly Still

In the evening quiet
a spring sun high,
light winds nearly silent.

In the distance
a sailboat, anchor dropped,
unmoving.

Clouds resting over the mountains
on the far side of the water,
still, or appear to be.

Hovering clouds, determined
to stay in their chosen spot,
hugging the mountain, as if for comfort.

Songs Rising

She said she saw a wren
sitting on a branch
and singing.

She said the song was sweet
like a prayer
rising on air.

Bird prayers rising on air
toward Heaven.

Now, when I hear birds sing,
I remember her words.

That some of the songs
rising on air
are prayers.

For birds
and for all of the earth.

Grateful, that among them,
among the many notes rising,
is my name.

Meditation

Almost mid-June
yet windy and cold.
Appropriate weather
for melancholy.

On the beach I come again to be among them.
The long-necked colony of Cormorants
on the abandoned pier.
Cut off from the shore and its busyness.

They rest in total silence
facing the open sea,
like a group
in deep meditation.

Maybe they are.
It is other-worldly here,
and so I come
for the Cormorants and their deep quiet.

They know me now.
Know I come for stillness, like themselves.
From the storms, the intrusions, of a very different world.

Fort Casey

The old fort's guns
have been silent
yet remain imposing
since World War I.

Still facing
the passage to the sea.
Sentinels of witness
for what could have been.

Now, week-end families
come for picnics and hikes.
The youngsters climb the cannons,
playing war games.

Strange. . . these grounds,
made for combat,
now echo with laughter
and the barking of dogs on a long leash.

I take pictures and sit on a footbridge,
grateful that this place,
now richly green,
never saw the horror of war.

The Squawkers

A steady rain falls
over the Cormorant Colony on the abandoned pier.
They remain
silent and stoic.

Soon the silence is broken.
The lone seagull,
I assumed to be a convert among Cormorants,
remains quiet.

Now, a new gull arrives,
rowdy and loud.
Enticing the other
to a shouting match.

The Cormorants, though, remain silent,
true to their nature;
appearing to ignore
the two carousers.

But, I don't like this!
I come here for quiet
and meditation,
away from noise.

Where are the Cormorant Police?
This will not stand!
After all, it only takes a couple of the loud and proud
to bring ruin to an entire neighborhood.

Kinship

Real kinship goes deep.
It touches the street sweeper,
and the loyal dog at my feet.
It touches the stately Douglas Fir,
and the waves of the expansive sea.
Touching even the king on his throne,
wondering who is real,
and who is not.

The Why

It's been two days.
And I've not returned to normal.
To where I was before
I went to get him.

The small baby rabbit
with the big doe eyes…
that I still picture after leaving him
at the animal hospital.

The lady who called my animal rescue group
had him in a box on a soft towel.
Her dog, following instinct, had caught him.
So, how can I blame him?

But, those doe eyes that I saw!
The innocence and trust as I rubbed his head,
deep and profound,
would not leave me.

I took a walk in the deep forest afterward.
Thank God for trees!
Where my questioning mind
quiets to silence.

I continue
to wrestle with
the many unanswered whys
in the world.

Many which
will not be answered
as long as I am
this side of heaven.

Here, for now,
again and again,
I surrender because
I must.

To the deep peace
of the embracing woods,
and the quiet of its long and continuous
unuttered sound.

To the Cormorants, Again

The minister gave his sermon.
And, it was good.

But, there are times
when the natural world
speaks more deeply
than words.

Again, I drive to the colony,
the very large colony
of Cormorants on
the old, abandoned pier.

And, again, I watch them
immersed in their deep silence,
facing the open water,
stoically.

The same penetrating silence that embraces.
Such that previous thoughts,
even the leaden and weighty of the earth's very survival,
drift upward and away, like mist …over the top of the
    trees.

Whisper

That evening was soft and clear,
just a hint of chill.
Mountains stretching far
across the horizon.

Remembering the gratitude earlier
of shelter dogs being walked,
deep grateful eyes
and the soft sweep of tails.

Here next to the sea,
and alone,
all weighty thoughts fall
and lie down.

Dissolving in the granular moisture
of sand,
and the whisper
of sea and waves of foam.

Still

In a moment of grace,

a red-winged hawk

flew silently overhead,

wings outstretched,

while even the night wind,

overcome with awe,

held its breath . . .

Courtesy Jeff Danielson © 2025

About the Author

Reuben V. Greene III's writings come from explorations into the world of nature. Away from things fashioned by the hands of men. A stream, a towering tree in birdsong or a cloud drifting often speak beyond words...when one is quiet enough to hear. Quiet enough to feel the energy of these subtle healers. Since childhood, he has followed these voices.

With degrees in International Relations and History, he has traveled worldwide, continually in awe. Humbled by even the quietest and smallest of nature's vocabulary.

These are great conversations...even those without vocal response. Conversations that continually exhilarate, rendering one more clear-eyed and appreciative regarding earth's unending gifts. And the need to protect them.

In so doing, we ensure that we protect our own precious planet, but perhaps worlds beyond and vaster than our own imaginations.

$16.95
ISBN 979-8-9862415-3-1

www.ingramcontent.com/pod-product-compliance
Lightning Source LLC
Chambersburg PA
CBHW020514030426
42337CB00011B/376